Original title:
The Ocean's Hidden Treasure

Copyright © 2025 Creative Arts Management OÜ
All rights reserved.

Author: Miriam Kensington
ISBN HARDBACK: 978-1-80587-369-3
ISBN PAPERBACK: 978-1-80587-839-1

Encounters in the Abyss

In the deep where fish wear hats,
There's a crab who dances with some gnats.
A whale with shades sings a tune,
While octopuses play peek-a-boo!

A treasure map made of jellyfish,
Best leads to a giant, wiggly dish.
Seaweed wraps like a fancy tie,
As seagulls giggle and wave goodbye.

Quests for Glittering Delights

Seeking sparkles like a pirate crew,
With dirty socks, oh, what a view!
A clam with pearls does a silly jig,
While dolphins toss a soggy twig.

They chase a ship made of candy bars,
Bumping into jellyfish with silly scars.
A treasure chest? Just a box of fries,
With soggy bread and one big surprise!

Shadows of the Enchanted Sea

In shadows where the mermaids prance,
They throw a party, a fishy dance.
A trumpet fish plays a funky beat,
While shrimps perform in tap shoes on their feet.

There's giggles from a sunken shoe,
Holding stories of an old sea crew.
With love letters sealed by barnacle glue,
And a goldfish dreaming of a mermaid stew.

Underwater Whispers of Time

The turtlenecks whisper ancient tales,
While starfish debate the best of sails.
A playful bubble just wants to pop,
And catches a seahorse doing the flop.

Old bottles drift with secrets to share,
But who reads the labels? No one's aware.
A treasure of giggles, a bounty of screams,
In the depths of the sea, where laughter beams.

Waters that Hold Secrets

In waves that whisper silly tunes,
Fish dance with hats and spoons.
Octopuses tell jokes so bright,
Crabs compete in a waddle fight.

A treasure chest? No, just some snacks,
With gummy worms and seaweed hacks.
The turtles chuckle, having their fun,
While dolphins jump, saying, 'We're number one!'

The Pirate's Dream

Yo ho ho, a pirate's plight,
Searching for gold in the moonlight.
But he finds a chest of rubber ducks,
And pirate hats made of old fire trucks.

'Where's the loot?' he shouts in glee,
As seagulls laugh and sing for free.
He sails away with a squeaky grin,
His treasure hunt, just a comical spin.

Beneath the Blue Veil

Under the waves where laughter flows,
Live fish that wear flashy clothes.
Seahorses snicker, playing a game,
While starfish applaud, calling their name.

A diver swims in a flipper parade,
With jellyfish joining, a quirky brigade.
Bubbles burst with giggles, oh what a sight,
As clams wink, 'Is this day or night?'

Glimmers at Dusk

At dusk, the waves twinkle in hue,
Where sea creatures attempt a debut.
A fish in a bow tie, looking so slick,
Says, 'Let's have a show, oh quick, quick, quick!'

They juggle pearls and do the cha-cha,
While a crab plays guitar, olé, olé, blah!
With laughter erupting from coral reefs,
The underwater party defies disbelief!

Riddles of the Brackish Pools

In waters murky, laughter bubbles,
A crab in a top hat grins and shuffles.
The fish wear ties, what a sight to see,
As they dance around like it's jubilee.

A clam tells jokes, his tongue unhinges,
While seaweed sways like it just enjoys fringes.
The splashes echo, a chorus so bright,
In brackish pools, they party all night.

Deposits of Time's Embrace

An old ship's captain with a penchant for pranks,
Hides his treasure behind ocean's banks.
But it's all just shells and some keys that don't fit,
While the mermaids giggle, they know, it's a skit.

The sands are laughing, they tickle your toes,
As sandcastles wobble, everyone knows.
A parrot squawks tales, his stories are grand,
But they're all bits of nonsense straight out of a band.

Guardians of the Nautical Realm

The octopus guards with eight juggling arms,
While turtles roll dice, spreading laughter like charms.
A dolphin flips high, with a wink and a grin,
As fish snap selfies, let the fun begin!

With sea urchins gossiping, spinning their tales,
And starfish trying to write down the scales.
The laughter is roaring, a wild, happy scene,
For hidden delights, they'll turn you quite green.

The Sunken Chronicles

In sunken ships, where treasures lie low,
The pirates left jokes, and a rubber chicken glow.
A bottle of giggles adrift in the tide,
In stories of sea, let hilarity slide.

Old maps scribbled with doodles and glee,
Marking locations where all the fish flee.
As the waves tell secrets and tickle the past,
The joy of the sea, a spell ever cast.

Lost Kingdoms of the Deep

In a castle made of seaweed,
The fish all dance and play,
The crab is quite the ruler,
He loves to sing all day.

Mermaids wear socks made of pearls,
While dolphins flip and dive,
A turtle shouts, "I'm the queen!"
And all the sea stars thrive.

An octopus is the chef,
He cooks up jelly stew,
He says, "It's what I can do,
With eight arms, it's not new!"

But pirates roam with treasure maps,
In search of fishy gold,
They end up with just seaweed,
And stories never told.

Echoes of the Ocean Floor

Bubbles float with gossip flies,
Shells whisper tales of old,
The clams play secret charades,
While sea cucumbers are bold.

Anemones wear silly hats,
That look like made of foam,
The starfish laugh in unison,
"This is our underwater home!"

A dancing shrimp is DJ now,
With beats that shake the reef,
The sea sponges groove along,
In rhythmic disbelief.

But when the net comes swooping down,
They all begin to shout,
"Run for your squishy lives, folks,
It's a seafood takeout!"

Murmurs in the Brine

The lobsters throw a masquerade,
With fins and tails galore,
The seaweed twirls like crazy,
While jellyfish hit the floor.

Seahorses play peek-a-boo,
Amongst the coral walls,
"Oh look, there's my cousin!"
Squeaks one, as laughter calls.

A sea urchin spins a yarn,
About a whale who flew,
"From barnacles to clouds, my friends,
The tales just grew and grew!"

And when the tide comes rolling in,
The party starts to fade,
The fish all head back home,
To dream of their escapade.

The Sapphire's Silent Song

A sapphire secret softly hums,
Beneath the waves so blue,
The fish all nod and wink,
And share a laugh or two.

A flounder plays the piano,
With flippers deft and spry,
But the mermaid steals the show,
As she starts to fly high.

A crab with shades struts along,
With swagger, oh so grand,
He shouts, "Life is just a dance,
With rhythms of the sand!"

But as the tide begins to turn,
The bubbles bubble up,
And all the songs turn gibberish,
In laughter, they all sup!

Treasures of the Deep Blue

Beneath the waves where fish do scoff,
A pirate's sock is what they toss.
With shiny shells and bits of gold,
They trade the tales that never get old.

A crab in shades — a fashion flair,
Wearing sunglasses, without a care.
While dolphins dance, they leap and dive,
Claiming they're the best alive!

A sunken ship with moldy bread,
The captain's toast, he must have read.
Mermaids laugh and pinch their cheeks,
Sharing secrets with the clams that speak.

So grab your map and don your fins,
Join in the fun where laughter wins!
With treasures found and joy anew,
Underwater, a grand view!

Glittering Gems in the Sand

The beach is filled with sparkly things,
A flip-flop worn by laughing kings.
With jellyfish doing silly flips,
And seagulls snatching our potato chips.

Shells that gleam like rainbow candy,
Seashells arguing — isn't that dandy?
A treasure map drawn in ketchup red,
A search for goldfish — or just some bread!

Starfish posing like movie stars,
Complaining there are too many cars.
While crabs hold a dance-off on the shore,
Who knew beach life could be such a chore?

With treasures made of giggles and fun,
Digging for laughter — we have begun!
In warm sunlight, the day feels grand,
While silly critters occupy the sand!

The Cradle of Nautical Dreams

In night's embrace, the waves they sway,
A boat of dreams floats far away.
With fish wearing hats, oh what a sight,
As sailors snore through the starry night.

Octopuses playing cards below,
With jellybeans, their stakes do grow.
A whale sings tunes that's quite off-key,
While laughing mermaids sip cold tea.

Ghost ships linger, with silly pranks,
Blowing bubbles as the crew swanks.
With treasure maps covered in jam,
The crew now searches for breakfast ham!

The sea's a playground for all who roam,
Where laughter and mischief feel like home.
With giggles and dreams that softly steam,
In the cradle of waves, we find our dream!

Where Lost Ships Whisper

In the fog, where secrets lie,
Ghost ships wander, oh me, oh my!
With whispers sweet, they tell their tale,
Of sailors' socks that went to sail.

Mermaids trade old grumpy tales,
Of barnacles and fishy gales.
A shipwrecked captain's broken clock,
Says time's a joke and laughs in shock!

Treasure chests filled with rubber ducks,
Forgotten dreams and silly bucks.
A parrot squawks and steals a snack,
Claiming goldfish is what he'd lack!

The ocean sings, a mystery spun,
With laughter, adventures, all in fun.
For in every bubble and wave that flirts,
A treasure of joy and laughter lurks!

Tides of Buried Truth

Down below where bubbles rise,
A pirate's gold is not so wise.
For every chest, a rusty key,
And maps that lead to lost TV!

The gulls all laugh and squawk with glee,
As sailors search, their hair a spree.
"X" marks the spot, but wait, oh dear!
It's where I buried my last beer!

With treasure hunts that last for days,
They hope to find the fish that prays.
But all they get is stinky socks,
And used-up bait in rusty box!

So, heed the waves, enjoy your fate,
The true treasure's a first-rate mate.
For laughter's worth much more than cash,
At least, until your boat does crash!

Dances of Dolphins and Treasures

Oh, the dolphins dance so bright,
In waters clear, pure delight.
They twirl and flip with such a flair,
While munching snacks, we stand and stare.

With every splash, they seem to say,
"No gold for you; just join the play!"
A treasure hunt for silly hats,
And seaweed wigs—they're cool, not brats!

In the midst of all this fun,
A crab does race, and what a run!
He claims the chest, he's won the prize,
But opens it, and finds no fries!

So here's a toast to fins and flops,
To laughter that never stops.
In frothy waves, we'll join the ball,
The true gold's in fun for all!

Castaway Dreams in the Deep

On a raft of dreams, they float so bold,
    Eating coconuts, claiming gold.
"Where's the treasure?" one must shout,
    While all that's left is crumbs, no doubt!

With fish that giggle and shells that sing,
    They stumble through this pirate fling.
With snickers loud, they raise their cup,
    To toast the plunder, uh-oh, whoops up!

A mermaid waves, and what a sight!
    "Treasure? Nope, just sheer delight!"
With fins that sparkle, laughter beams,
    Their prize is found in funny dreams.

Yet under stars, they gaze and sigh,
    Wishing for treasure, oh me—oh my!
But as the waves pull them away,
    They find their joy in wacky play!

Voyage of the Battered Hull

A ship with patches, brimming with zest,
Sets sail to find what's deemed the best.
But hold on tight—what's this, a bump?
A treasure chest or just a thump?

With teams of jesters manning the deck,
They search for loot on the wild speck.
But every wave brings wobbly fun,
And tattered sails beneath the sun.

A parrot squawks, "You won't regret!"
As they dive in to find the best bet.
With muddy boots, they start to dig,
Only to find an old, wet wig!

Yet laughter rings on this quirky quest,
For friendship makes them feel the best.
Who needs riches when fun is gold?
In every chuckle, tales unfold!

Enigmas of the Sea Floor

Bubbles rise like secrets told,
Shiny things in sand and cold.
Starfish giggle, crabs do dance,
Who knew riches hid by chance?

A pirate's map, a fishy joke,
With every wave, the laughter spoke.
Seashells sing a silly tune,
As dolphins play beneath the moon.

Octopus wears a fancy hat,
He waves to fishes, 'How 'bout that?'
Underwater parties, what a sight,
Seaweed dancing, it's pure delight!

Gems misplaced with every tide,
Lost in skips and ocean glide.
Treasure chests of goofy finds,
Each dive reveals what fate unwinds.

Hidden Riches in the Foam

Foamy waves bring tales anew,
Of goldfish dreams and a pirate crew.
Sand dollars laugh at sandy feet,
They chuckle softly, what a treat!

Seagulls swoop to steal a fry,
While treasure chests wave hello, oh my!
A map drawn in ketchup on a bun,
As beach folks shout, 'Let's go for fun!'

Crabs hold conferences, what a sight,
Debating if the tide is right.
A hidden pearl, oh what a tease,
Shiny treasure found amidst the breeze!

Shells are hosts to parties galore,
With conchs providing music at the shore.
Ocean's whims, so droll and grand,
Where silly dreams wash up on sand.

Nautical Whispers

Whispers float on salty air,
Jellyfish gossip, unaware.
Barnacles boast of life so fine,
While clams just grin at the ocean's twine.

Lobsters play tag in their own lair,
With stretchy arms, they nearly tear!
Pirates hiccup, chugging grog,
As fish swim by, they dance and jog.

A whale is spinning tales so vast,
Of treasure lost and friendships cast.
Mermaid laughter fills the night,
In the murky depths, it's pure delight!

Squids compete to draw a crowd,
In colors bright, they're feeling proud.
Ocean's secrets, giggles rise,
With every wave, new fun surprise.

Guardians of the Lost Depths

Guardian fish in armor bright,
Guarding treasures out of sight.
They wear crowns of seaweed greens,
While plotting wild, whimsical scenes.

Turtles sing, "We're not so slow,
Just taking time with our treasure show!"
Starfish plan a heist for fun,
For hidden gems, they'll never run!

Clams with pearls in shades of pink,
Giggle softly, "What do you think?"
Octopi pose for ocean films,
In search of treasure, they're the whims!

With waves as their own silly guide,
They hunt for wonders, full of pride.
What fun it is beneath the tides,
Where laughter flows and treasure hides!

Ancient Whispers in Saltwater

Beneath the waves where secrets flow,
A crab in a sombrero steals the show.
With hints of gold and tales so grand,
He dances a jig on the soft, warm sand.

Fish trade gossip like sailors of old,
A sea turtle's story is worth its weight in gold.
Octopuses juggle with quite the flair,
As dolphins burst forth with laughter to share.

Barnacles gossip on a shipwrecked shoe,
"Was that a pirate, or just a stew?"
Mermaids chuckle and flip their tails,
While seagulls squawk out their hearty sales.

With oceanside antics, joy's a sure bet,
As crabs compete in a dash for the wet.
With treasures of laughter, not gold or gems,
The salty delight of friends and their hem.

So dive into giggles, let worries cease,
In depths of the water, find riotous peace.
For beneath the surface, where laughter swells,
The tides bring forth tales that the sea gladly tells.

A Pearl in the Abyss

In the depths where fish do grin,
A clam sings loud, it's quite a din.
With pearls so shiny, they tease and dance,
Making wave-washed sand take a chance.

A crab dressed up in a glittery coat,
Claims he's a prince on a treasure boat.
While starfish giggle at his grand parade,
As shells blow kisses in every shade.

A dolphin's joke makes the octopus blush,
Tickling fish as they start to rush.
With currents swaying, they twist and twine,
Even the seaweed thinks it's divine.

So if you wander where the wild waves play,
Look for the laughter beneath the spray.
For treasures gleam not just in gold,
But in the stories of joy retold.

Sirens of Sunken Secrets

Beneath the waves where secrets sleep,
Mermaids giggle, their laughter deep.
They count old coins and ancient rings,
While singing silly, off-key flings.

A shipwreck's a party of sorts, you see,
With fish doing the cha-cha and an octopus DJ.
As bubbles float up to pop with a cheer,
Even the crabs gather 'round for a beer.

A treasure map made of gummy treats,
Leads them to candy beneath their seats.
With jellyfish waltzing in cotton candy swirls,
The ocean's a rave for all of them girls!

So if you hear tunes from below the blue,
Just know it's the sirens inviting you too.
To join their dance in the treasure parade,
Where fun is the fortune that they've made!

Coral Gardens of Enchantment

In gardens where the corals gleam,
Fish wear hats, it's quite the dream.
With dancing anemones waving high,
As clowns make faces that make you sigh.

A turtle in shades moves slow and wise,
While jellybeans swim to surprise the eyes.
With sea cucumbers putting on a show,
They strut and parade, all in a row.

Sea urchins giggle, their spikes all a-flick,
As schools of minnows perform the trick.
The ocean floor hosts a beauty parade,
With every splash, a new joke is laid.

So dive down deep to find the fun,
In coral gardens under the sun.
Where laughter bubbles and treasures unfold,
It's a whimsical world, bright and bold!

Beneath the Moonlit Waters

When moonlight dances on the sea's embrace,
Fish wear pajamas, a curious case.
A lobster's wearing slippers, oh so bright,
While a seahorse takes a snooze, what a sight!

The waves whisper secrets that tickle the ear,
With giggles echoing, can you hear?
Octopus juggling, so sly and spry,
While a kite-fish flutters in the night sky.

A treasure chest holds snacks galore,
With gummy worms shouting, 'Just one more!'
As anglerfish flash their silly lights,
Telling jokes to the star-fish all night.

So come take a plunge when the stars appear,
For laughter bursts forth with every cheer.
In the depths of fun where the treasures play,
The ocean's magic makes silly sway.

Pure Essence of the Deep

In the depths where fish do play,
A pirate's sock lost yesterday.
Shiny coins that glitter still,
A clam that sings, what a big thrill!

A sunken chest, all full of pants,
Mermaids dance in funny prance.
Jellyfish in disco lights,
Who knew sea life could be quite a sight!

Octopus with eight great arms,
Catching crabs with silly charms.
He offers me a seaweed snack,
I think I'll pass, I'll head back!

Bubbles rise, a treasure map,
Marked with fish who love to nap.
But under waves, oh what a mess,
Too much treasure means more stress!

Beneath the Celestial Waves

Underneath the bright moonlight,
Seahorses ride their bikes at night.
Starfish playing hopscotch too,
What a sight, I thought 'who knew?'

A pirate with a fishy hat,
Tripped on crabs—oh, fancy that!
His parrot squawks, 'You look a clown!'
Sinks into sand—it's quite the frown!

Turtles spinning past like tops,
Singing songs with funny hops.
They throw a party for the shells,
Pasta made from ocean gels!

Surprises hide in every nook,
An octopus reads a funny book.
Under waves, the fun won't cease,
Each dive is filled with silly peace!

Whispers Beneath the Waves

Bubbles whisper secrets low,
A lost shoe? Oh, where'd it go?
Nemo's got a silly joke,
While seahorses giggle and poke.

Coral reefs hold strange delights,
Starfish wearing funny tights.
Clams that yodel, fish that sing,
Underwater make-believe spring!

A crab plays cards, he's quite a hoot,
Challenging turtles to a loot.
But when he loses, oh the fuss,
He tosses shells; it's all a plus!

"Join our game!" the dolphins cry,
"Bring your flippers, give it a try!"
Laughter echoes far and wide,
In hidden nooks where humor hides!

Secrets of the Tidal Depths

Down below where bubbles bloom,
Fish are huddled in a room.
They share tales of treasures vast,
One dropped a sock, what a blast!

A clam with glasses tells a tale,
Of jellybeans that swim the scale.
"Don't eat me!" cries a flustered shrimp,
While seaweed does a jig and limp.

An octopus who plays guitar,
Strums a tune from right afar.
Squid join in with silly dance,
They made a splash—what a chance!

Hidden gems in every cove,
Laughter echoes, the sea's sweet grove.
Pirates chuckle with fishy friends,
In the depths where the fun never ends!

Tales from the Deep Blue Caverns

In caverns deep where fishes dance,
A crab wore shoes, just took a chance.
He strutted 'round with quite a flair,
    As octopi pulled at their hair.

A whale told jokes; they rolled with glee,
A sportier wave than you might see.
But when he laughed, the bubbles flew,
    And tangled all his friends in goo!

A starfish played the ukulele,
Strumming chords while feeling sprightly.
His tunes were catchy, made fish sway,
But offbeat shells kept swimming away!

In these strange depths, laughter flows,
Where clownfish giggle, everyone knows.
For treasures found don't gleam or shine,
    It's joy that sparkles, oh so divine!

Beneath Waves of Time

Sea turtles gossip about their day,
One's got a secret—he's on a diet!
Another's on a quest for pearls,
But ends up munching seaweed twirls.

A dolphin swam with popcorn flair,
Spraying kernels here and there.
The seagulls came, much to his plight,
"Stop tossing snacks! It's not polite!"

In sunken ships, they play hide and seek,
With mermaids laughing, hiding meek.
Their voices echo through the deep,
While lost old sailors snore and weep.

But treasures buried, they've found a trick,
They take a selfie—click! Click! Click!
For humor's gold is worth much more,
Than all the gems on any shore!

Nautical Echoes and Tales Untold

A fish in glasses thinks he's wise,
He claims to know all ocean lies.
But when a shark asks where's the pearl,
He simply blinks and starts to twirl.

A mermaid swims with rainbow hair,
Singing gently, filling the air.
But every note attracts a crowd,
The fish all cheer and sing out loud!

A crab with dreams of popping fame,
Wants to run in the nautical game.
With tiny legs, he gives a show,
But trips on seaweed—oh no, oh no!

In shallow tides where laughter's churned,
Time's charm is found—no need to yearn.
Where echoes ring like bubbles burst,
Here tales unfold, and joys are first!

Crystals in the Foam

A jellyfish danced with glimmering lights,
She skipped on waves through starry nights.
But every flip, she'd lose her glow,
And blame the tide for her bad show.

A shrimp with goggles swam so spry,
He mimicked whales with a silly cry.
But when he leapt, his stance went wrong,
And belly-flopped—it was quite the song!

The clams held meetings without a care,
Arguing 'bout who had the flair.
But all were dressed in bubbles grand,
A crystal ball in each little hand!

So dive into fun, where treasures gleam,
Not just in riches, but in the dream.
For laughter's gem in each foam's swirl,
Is worth more than all, oh what a pearl!

Lost Chill of Waves

A clam was caught in quite a freeze,
He shivered in his shell with ease.
A fish with shades swam by in style,
"Brr! You need a towel!" he said with a smile.

A crab danced in his pincer shoes,
While seahorses laughed at his snooze.
"You lost your chill, you silly mate!"
The wave said, "Don't worry, just wait!"

A dolphin flipped, it seemed so grand,
While jellyfish swayed to the band.
"Come join the fun, it's warm and bright!"
But clam just shivered, still cold as night.

Then sunbeams broke through, oh what a sight!
The clam woke up, said, "Now that's right!"
With laughter spread across the bay,
He danced along, chasing chill away!

Gold beneath the Salted Surface

There's a tale of fish who sold their bling,
A sardine sporting a diamond ring.
A crab said, "Fella, you're quite a sight!"
"Well, darling, it's good to be bright!"

The starfish laughed with envy in tow,
"I'm just a star, but I want to glow!"
But pearls were hidden all over the bed,
Cranky old barnacles shook their dread.

An octopus laughed, "I've got more arms!"
"Gold's no big deal, it loses its charms!"
Yet sadly he fished for trinket games,
While fish paraded around with their names.

"Oh my! What a shiny, wobbly mess!"
Cried a guppy in a sparkly dress.
All treasure hunters begin to frolic,
As laughter echoed; life was just comical.

Treasures Cradled by Currents

A treasure map drawn in ink so blue,
Leads to secrets too wild to pursue.
A dolphin kept giggling, swam round and round,
"Let's dig for treasures that can't be found!"

A pirate parrot squawked with glee,
"Where's that gold? It must be for me!"
But all he found was an old shoe,
"Ah, perfect!" he cried, "Now two's a crew!"

The currents swirled and couldn't decide,
What to keep and what to hide.
A floppy old boot floated by with flair,
"Gold is nice, but I'm a collector of air!"

With giggles and splashes, the tide would tease,
While treasure seekers searched with ease.
A compass spun, like a kite in the breeze,
Finding true wealth in giggles and cheese!

Fables of the Coral Kingdom

In the kingdom of coral, where bright colors flow,
A clownfish swirled with quite a show.
He told a tall tale of sharks with wings,
While shrimps did the dance, all wearing bling.

A hermit crab limped with marvelous flair,
His house was a bottle he'd find anywhere.
"Watch me boogie, just strike a pose!"
The coral reef giggled, 'What a funny nose!'

The sea turtle yawned and flipped with ease,
"Your stories are wild, like such a tease!"
Time ticked slowly as they giggled and sang,
In a bubblegum world, where laughter rang.

So whenever you visit those waves with cheer,
Remember the fables from under the sphere.
For treasures aren't gold or shiny bright things,
But joy and laughter that true friendship brings!

Echoes from the Shell-Strewn Beach

Crabs in bow ties dancing round,
They argue who's the silliest clown.
Seagulls squawk with all their might,
While fish joke about the best flight.

Sandy castles fall with a thud,
As little frogs swim in the mud.
A starfish wearing shades so neat,
Claims it's tough on this hot seat.

Buckets brim with treasures bright,
Looks like a glowing episode of fright.
A conch shell sings a silly tune,
While turtles laugh, and the crabs swoon.

The sun sets down, a splendid sight,
On a beach where giggles ignite.
And all the seashells wear a grin,
As night falls; let the fun begin.

Hushed Voices of the Deep

Whales whisper secrets in the blue,
About the fish that dance and chew.
Octopuses play hide and seek,
While pufferfish make faces unique.

Turtles wear their sailor hats,
And tease the dolphins, "You're all acrobats!"
Anemones laugh with squeaky glee,
As they play catch with a lost key.

Bubbles rise with giggles and gaff,
They tickle the seaweed, oh what a laugh!
A clam tells jokes that fall with a splash,
As colorful fish create a big flash.

And when the tides begin to sway,
The ocean sings, "Come dance and play!"
Submerged in fun, with chortles deep,
In this realm of secrets we keep.

Mystique of the Hidden Lagoon

A hidden pond, with frogs in tow,
They croak in rhymes, putting on a show.
Lily pads become the stage,
Where fish recite poetry of the age.

A treasure chest with rubber ducks,
Filled with giggles, and just our luck!
Crickets chirp in vibrant tune,
As the moon peeks in, a funny boon.

The snails wear bling from past escapades,
While turtles joke about their charades.
Pond scum jokes float through the air,
"All of you are such a silly pair!"

As night approaches, tales unfold,
Of caverns deep and treasures bold.
In this lagoon, we laugh and play,
Where the funny creatures come to stay.

Nature's Lost Artifacts

A bottle corked with laughter loud,
Unleashed a wave, a giggling crowd.
Seashells feel like ancient kings,
While old boots tell tales of strange flings.

A compass spins like it's bewildered,
And seaweed whispers, "No need to be tethered."
Jellyfish wear glow-in-the-dark shoes,
Strolling around with nothing to lose.

A shipwreck's pride is all rusted gold,
With pirates who've gotten rather old.
They joke of journeys, oh what a spree,
Of treasure maps, lost at sea!

With every wave that cracks and breaks,
History laughs, and nature quakes.
In this wild, wacky ocean space,
Funny moments always leave a trace.

Abyssal Wonders Unveiled

Beneath the waves, a shoe was found,
It wiggled, squiggled, danced around.
A fish claimed it as its own,
Now it's the star, all alone.

Jellyfish wear hats for style,
Squid laugh at their own long wile.
Octopuses juggle with great flair,
While sea cucumbers just don't care.

Crabs sneak in a game of tag,
While dolphins jump, wagging their flags.
With every splash, a giggle rises,
Who needs pearls when you've got surprises?

So, dive down deep, take a look,
You might find treasures in every nook.
From funny hats to dancing shoes,
In azure depths, it's all good news!

Legends of the Blue Horizon

Mermaids knit with fishing line,
While seagulls squawk, 'It's snack time!'
A whale hums tunes with pop and fizz,
What a life—oh, how it whizzes!

Giant clams host tea parties grand,
With starfish cookies, oh so sand.
Turtles arrive in speedy haste,
Bringing punch, oh what a taste!

The kraken spins tales of past fights,
While shrimp trade gossip through the nights.
Anemones showing off their hues,
They all giggle—oh, what a snooze!

Beneath the blue, a joyful spree,
Who knew fish could laugh with glee?
So raise a glass, let's toast our plight,
In this splashy world of pure delight!

A Dive into Serenity

At the reef, the colors shine,
A lobster's dressed in bright design.
With shades and hats, they strut their stuff,
Critters great and small—oh, how tough!

Disco fish throw parties at dawn,
While crabs do the cha-cha, just carry on.
Starfish take selfies, don't be shy,
As bubbles rise—oh me, oh my!

A pufferfish deflates for a giggle,
While clownfish make a silly wiggle.
Coral castles made of sponge,
Are home to a sea snail that loves to plunge.

So dive on in, let worries cease,
With every splash, find joy and peace.
Under the waves, the fun just grows,
In the sea's embrace, let laughter flow!

Reflections on Liquid Jewels

In tidal pools, the mischief stirs,
Where sea urchins wear fuzzy furs.
A school of fish wearing bowties bright,
Swim through bubbles, oh what a sight!

The tides sing songs of playful pranks,
As sea horses line up in cool flanks.
With every wave, a giggle forms,
As barnacles dance through salty storms.

Gulls gather 'round for a comedy show,
While jellyfish juggle in the flow.
An octopus sips on seaweed tea,
Laughing at what a sight it be!

So here's to the gems tucked deep below,
With laughter and cheer, let the good times flow.
With every splash and playful tease,
Life in the blue is bound to please!

The Sea's Buried Charms

Beneath the waves, a treasure trove,
Where mermaids dance and sea dogs rove.
A goldfish sings, a crab does prance,
While clams hold secrets, thrilled by chance.

With sunken ships and boots askew,
A pirate's hat sticks out in view.
A treasure map marked off with fries,
The seagulls laugh and steal your pies.

An octopus in a sailor's hat,
Conducts a band of fish, imagine that!
With a wink and a jig, they sway so grand,
While treasure seekers shrug, "Oh, isn't it bland?"

With bubbles rising, a treasure chest,
Full of odd socks—the ocean's jest!
In this watery world where giggles abound,
The real treasure's a laugh, not a pearl to be found.

Tides Carrying Secrets

The tide rolls in with a goofy grin,
Whispers of secrets hiding within.
A fish with a mustache swims near a rock,
Telling tall tales of an old tick-tock.

A sandcastle crumbles in the best way,
It rears up high, then says, "No way!"
The barnacles chuckle, the seashells stare,
As sea cucumbers wiggle with flair.

A crab in a tux offers a toast,
To seashells and sea snails, they brag the most.
With each wave comes a joke on repeat,
Did you hear about the clam who knew how to cheat?

As kelp sways to some underwater beat,
A dolphin giggles; it can't be beat!
With tides carrying secrets, oh what a sight,
Laughing at fish, dancing mid-flight.

Glances at the Drowned Past

A ship in a bottle, or so it seems,
Is filled with memories, dreams, and beams.
A parrot squawks tales of old derring-do,
As snails get mad, saying, "We knew you!"

Historic anchors with stories to tell,
Of fishy romances that didn't end well.
A whale plays cards with a cheeky shark,
Both laughing about a treasure map and a park.

A rusted sword makes a great floor mat,
While starfish gossip about the cool cat.
With hikes on the seafloor, the laughter rings loud,
Echoing tales that've made the sea proud.

With glances back at a time long gone,
Where eel wrestlers faced the dawn.
The drowned past giggles, quite a fuss,
For who knew the sea could be this humorous?

Gems of the Forgotten Waters

In forgotten waters, gems lay still,
With bubbles of laughter, what a thrill!
A pirate's tooth, shiny and bright,
Winks to a fish that's quite out of sight.

A conch shell boasts of its grand career,
As it tells corny jokes to all who can hear.
While pearls roll eyes at the shrimp's tall claims,
"Have you seen my bling? I'm rich in frames!"

A treasure chest filled with socks and shoes,
The underwater fashion? Quite the ruse!
With mermaids giggling at the seaweed style,
They twirl and dance, having fun all the while.

Among gems of laughter, the sea turns its key,
Unlocking fun for all, just wait and see.
For what's hidden below is often the best,
In quirky treasures, it's all just a jest!

Waters Holding Stories Untold

Bubbles giggle, fish do dance,
A crab wearing glasses, takes a glance.
Seashells whisper secrets near,
As barnacles laugh with glee, oh dear!

A pirate's sock floats by in style,
It's been lost for quite a while.
Mermaids trade old tales for pearls,
While jellyfish sway, giving twirls.

A sunken boot holds tales of shoe,
Of a sailor whose dream was to cook stew.
A treasure chest with nothing but snacks,
Turns out the treasure is just some chips and cracks!

Starfish applaud, the sea weaves fun,
With all its treasures under the sun.
Under waves, laughter's the catch,
In every corner, stories match!

Once Lost, Now Found Underwater

A rubber ducky found quite a fleet,
Sailing around on fins, oh so sweet.
He floats with poise, feeling quite grand,
In the soggy shores of a seaweed land.

Tales of socks and lunch meat in tow,
All the stuff that poor divers' know.
Puddles laugh, while fish hold a show,
"Who needs gold when there's laughter to throw?"

A spoon sings a tune, quite out of tune,
With a flounder who's dancing, none too soon.
They're all rooting for the lost, found gnome,
Who prefers his old life, way down home!

What unity lies in the briny blue,
A circus of fun, with a crew so true.
All the lost things celebrate their fate,
For underwater life is just first-rate!

Moonlit Discoveries

Under moonlight, fishes wear hats,
While octopuses dance with their spats.
Waves chuckle softly at the scene,
As shadows of treasure get a sheen.

A rusty bell rings out, so odd,
"Who knew the sea was such a fraud?"
A crab plays poker with a snail,
With kelp as chips, they never fail.

Seahorses take turns on a slide,
While starfish cheer and swell with pride.
The jewel of the deep is wild and free,
With hidden wonders just waiting to see!

In this playful kingdom, so ripe with fun,
Even the seaweed wants to run.
For treasures found on this moonlit shore,
Are laughter and joy, who could ask for more?

Treasures of the Forgotten Depths

A tricycle sunk, what a sight!
With fish taking turns, pure delight.
"Who lost this?" they ponder and muse,
While exploring their world with funny views.

Old boots hold stories of squishy sand,
As turtles giggle, oh isn't it grand?
A treasure chest full of colorful snacks,
For sea critters' parties, that's how the facts!

SpongeBob's cousin sways with glee,
Best fishing buddy, can you see?
A bottle floats, a message in jest,
"Help, I'm trapped in a seafood fest!"

With each dive down, joy is uncovered,
Quirky treasures make hearts discover.
In the depths, where laughter streams,
It's the underwater world of zany dreams.

Echoes of the Forgotten Shore

On the beach, I found a shoe,
Its mate was probably on a cruise.
Crabs threw a party, dancing in glee,
Hoping to catch a fish—just me!

Seagulls squawked like they knew it all,
Screaming insults, having a ball.
Tides brought in snacks, both salty and sweet,
The sand was a feast—what a treat!

A message in a bottle caught my eye,
But it was just a note from a pie.
"Help, I'm trapped in the crust!," it said,
I laughed so hard, fell back, and fed.

So next time you trip on a tossed-aside sock,
Remember it's not just a rock.
Dig through the beach, strike it rich,
Or find a flip-flop—make a new pitch!

Sunken Gemstones in the Sand

A treasure chest washed up today,
Alas! Just snails in a fray.
They glittered like pearls, all polished and fine,
But the only value was their slow, slimy line.

I spied a goldfish, with a crown on its head,
Claimed it ruled the waves from its seaweed bed.
The fish flicked its tail, gave me a nod,
But slipped out of sight, like an oceanic fraud.

With shovels in hand, my friends and I dug,
Found a plastic sword and a very old mug.
"X" marked a spot—oh, what a joke,
Now we're fans of dinnerware made of oak!

As the sunset painted the sky a nice hue,
We cheered for the finds, some old and some new.
Worth more than jewels? The laughter and fun,
Who needs a fortune when you've got sun?

Mysteries Adrift

A rubber duck sailed, lost in the foam,
Searching for friends, far from its home.
With a quack and a splash, it began to explore,
Where is the party? Just me on the shore!

Bottles bobbed by, with secrets inside,
One held a note: "Your hair's got great pride!"
A fish in a tux echoed slurs and shouts,
Claiming it was the gossip of the route.

I found some seaweed that looked quite posh,
Dressed up as a coat, with a fashionable swash.
Oh, the mysteries woven in seagrass and tide,
Most are just silliness, where fun takes a ride!

So raise up your toes and wiggle them free,
As we dance with the waves in silly glee.
Let the sea's funny tales lead you along,
Through fables of laughter, that's where we belong!

The Siren's Silent Song

A siren sat quietly, sipping her tea,
Where did her voice go? Oh, bother me!
She'd hum the old tunes, but lost all the notes,
Stuck choking on seaweed, that's what she wrote.

Fish gathered 'round for a raucous duet,
"Your serenade's worse than our last sunset!"
They flopped in approval, critiquing her flair,
But all she could do was pursed lips and glare.

A clam opened wide, surprised at the sound,
And the starfish lamented, "We're homeward bound!"
While dolphins giggled, plotting their joke,
A melody lost, but laughter bespoke!

So let's toast to sirens and tuneless glee,
For the quirkiest voices sing wild and free.
When songs are just chuckles, and joy is our goal,
We'll dance to the rhythm of the ocean's soul!

Shadows of the Coral Reefs

Beneath the waves, a crab with flair,
Dances like no one's watching there.
A fish in stripes, so bold, uncouth,
Claims he's a model, living truth.

A turtle sneezes, bubbles fly,
"Excuse me, folks!" it shrugs, oh my!
A dolphin laughs, flips with glee,
"Who needs a job? Just swim with me!"

Mysteries of the Water's Veil

A clam does yoga, perfect pose,
Right next to seaweed, no one knows.
A seahorse snickers at passing boats,
"Did you see that? They forgot their coats!"

Crabs play poker on the sandy floor,
Cheating, of course, they left the score.
The waves giggle, tickling the shore,
Telling secrets, wanting more!

Footprints on Forgotten Shores

A hermit crab wears a shiny shell,
Says, "I'm wealthy! Can you tell?"
But all he has is a pebble and stone,
His fashion choice is all his own.

Seagulls squawk jokes in the bright blue sky,
"Why did the fish fly? Oh my, oh my!"
They drop down snacks, a feast indeed,
While the sand collects what the tide freed.

The Keeper of the Sea's Bounty

An octopus juggles shiny things,
While the tangle of seaweed softly sings.
Starfish in hats cheer from afar,
"Best show in town! Come see, ajar!"

The wise old whale hums a tune,
While juggling clams beneath the moon.
"Life's a circus!" he lets out a roar,
As fish throw confetti, asking for more!

Shipwrecked Wonders

A ship once lost, a tale so bright,
With pirates' gold, tucked out of sight.
A parrot squawks, it steals the show,
While mermaids laugh and steal your toe!

The hull is home to a fishy crew,
With treasure maps drawn in squid ink blue.
They argue 'bout who gets the last shrimp,
While crabs do cartwheels—what a blimp!

A chest of socks, what a surprise!
Not gold or gems, just fishy ties.
The dolphins giggle, the seaweed sways,
As we treasure hunt in funny ways!

So if you're lost, don't shed a tear,
Just join the fish, and drink some beer.
For in this wreck, there's fun galore,
Who needs riches when you've got seashore!

Secrets in the Deep Blue

Bubbles rise, a secret's near,
A clam with pearls and a pint of beer.
Fish hold meetings, nibbling on kelp,
While sharks play cards, all quiet and stealth.

A sunken shoe, is that a sign?
Was it lost from a sailor's behind?
The octopus juggles, a real delight,
While sea turtles gossip under moonlight.

A treasure chest opens up with a gasp,
Filled with old jelly, and a moldy clasp.
Seahorses dance, wearing tiny hats,
Chasing old bubbles and pesky spats!

The sea cucumber jokes, slipping on sand,
Claiming he's tougher than any band.
Secrets shared, oh what a sight,
In the deep blue, everything's light!

The Dance of Forgotten Souls

Ghosts of sailors with silly grins,
They dance with fish, and wear old fins.
In the moonlight, they jig and twirl,
While crabs throw pearls, what a whirl!

One ghost shouts, "A toast, my friends!"
But spills his drink; the laughter never ends.
They spin around, a spectral band,
Lost 'neath the waves, but oh so grand!

They play a tune on a rusty shell,
With tunes that ring like a morning bell.
Invisible waltz, oh what a scene,
Beware of the jelly—they're not too keen!

So if you hear, beneath the waves,
The sounds of fools, and ghostly raves,
Join the dance, don't be afraid,
For laughter echoes where memories fade!

Beneath Starry Waves

In twilight waters, with sparkly light,
A fish in a tux takes a fancy flight.
Starfish giggle, with glitzy tights,
As they throw a party under starlit nights.

The seahorse DJ spins tunes with flair,
While clams hold high a seafood fair.
"Get your crab cakes, they're simply divine!"
Said one little fish, sipping briny wine.

An octopus juggles with jellyfish glee,
While starry eyes watch from coral tree.
Dolphins dive in, making big waves,
While sea urchins act like the chubby knaves!

So under the stars, in salty embrace,
Life is a party, a joyful race.
Treasure's not gold, not diamonds or pearls,
But laughter and fun in the ocean swirls!

The Lure of the Siren's Call

There once was a fish with big dreams,
He wished for a voice that could beam.
He tried to sing sweet,
But just made a feat,
And scattered the crowd with his screams.

A mermaid appeared with a grin,
She thought it was quite the whim.
With a twirl and a spin,
She laughed with a chin,
And taught him to dance like a fin.

Beneath the Surface Lies Gold

A crab found a coin in the mud,
He shouted, "Look here, I've struck a dud!"
But the other sea critters,
With their witty little flitters,
Just chuckled and swam in the flood.

He tried to recruit a wise whale,
"With this treasure, our legends will sail!"
But the whale just chortled,
As the crab felt thwarted,
"You're better off chasing a tail!"

Secrets Wrapped in Seaweed

There once was a clump of green strands,
That whispered of lost pirate lands.
With a plot and a wink,
Fish would gather and think,
Of treasures and fingers in bands.

But each time they went for the gold,
They found socks, bread, and tales retold.
With laughter, they'd bicker,
"What a great pick,
Next time let's stick to the mold!"

The Forgotten Fleet

A fleet of old boats lay aground,
With barnacles making their sound.
The captain, half-snoozing,
Was dreaming and losing,
His grip on the treasures he'd found.

As gulls made a ruckus and dive,
They spotted a sandwich alive!
With a feast on the deck,
They gave it a peck,
And claimed it was their lucky jive.

Shelters of Secrets in the Coral

In corals bright, where fish do hide,
A crab wears shoes, he's full of pride.
He struts around with flair and grace,
While seaweed giggles in its place.

A turtle laughs, his shell so round,
He bakes in sun, a sandy mound.
But watch out for the little shrimp,
Whose dance moves give the seas a limp!

A clownfish jokes, he's quite the wit,
With fins that flail, he won't just sit.
They all conspire, what a grand scheme,
To turn the reef into a dream!

So deep in hues, the colors bloom,
There's laughter here, not just a gloom.
In shelters bright, oh what a sight,
Coral's secrets bring pure delight!

A Journey to the Heart of the Sea

A dolphin dives with playful flair,
While bubbles pop without a care.
He twirls and spins, a joyful sight,
And tickles fish with pure delight.

A seahorse struts in regal pose,
With tiny tales that no one knows.
He tells a joke and lifts a fin,
The seaweed giggles, let's begin!

A starfish claims the best sun spot,
While barnacles plot, and tie the knot.
They whisper secrets, tales of glee,
In the deep blue, wild and free.

A journey here, a splash and dash,
Together we'll make quite the splash!
With every wave, such joy we see,
In the heart of this big ol' sea!

Siren's Gift Beneath the Currents

A siren sings from depths so low,
Her voice a comet, steal the show!
With fish all dancing in a trance,
They join her in a wiggly dance.

But wait! A lobster joins the crew,
He snaps his claws in time, who knew!
With crabs and eels, they start to jig,
Oh what a sight, this ocean gig!

A jellyfish floats, all aglow,
With wobbly moves, he steals the flow.
They share their gems, oh what a craze,
Underneath the waves, they sing their praise!

So if you hear a tune so sweet,
Just know that magic's at your feet.
While sirens smile beneath the waves,
It's joy not danger, in ocean caves!

Glimpses of Fauna Unseen

In shadows deep, where critters lurk,
A sneaky octopus goes to work.
He jumps from rocks, then winks an eye,
Behind the kelp, he's quite spry!

A fish in stripes, oh what a sight,
With jokes to share, he's full of might.
They swap tall tales of ocean fame,
As currents swirl, they stake their claim.

A sea cucumber stretches out wide,
Says, "Life's a journey, enjoy the ride!"
With every slip and slimy twist,
He shares a laugh, it can't be missed!

From gentle rays to playful seals,
In this world of joy, the heart reveals.
With glimpses of fauna, come and see,
The funny side of life beneath the sea!

Broken Bottles and Whispering Waves

In a bottle I found a note,
It said, 'Don't let the seagulls gloat!'
A fish swam by with a silly grin,
Said, 'I think your treasure's wearing thin!'

The sand's alive with a giggly sound,
As crabs do the cha-cha all around.
A turtle sat with a coral crown,
Sipping seaweed smoothies, feeling brown.

With every splash comes a squeaky joke,
Even starfish join in the poke.
An octopus juggled shells with flair,
While seaweed wiggles, joining the fair!

So bring your nets and zestful cheer,
For finding gold is never near.
Just laughter and waves in this wild spree,
That's the seashell's secret, come and see!

The Great Blue Mystery

What lurks beneath the playful foam?
A shoe? A sock? A lost ice cream cone?
With goggles on, it's time to dive,
To see if lost objects can come alive!

A fish in a tutu twirled with grace,
A crab named Carlos claimed his space.
"Don't let the currents steal my cheese!
I keep my stash where it's sure to please!"

Whales sing notes like exaggerated farts,
While dolphins play jazz with their charts.
I found a treasure—what joy it brings!
Just an old fork with enchanted strings!

So if you wander where the seaweed sways,
Expect silly things in wacky maze.
The deep's vast wonders are sure to impress,
For laughter's the loot that we can't suppress!

Crustaceans with Tales

In a burrow, crabs spin yarns so bright,
About a clam that danced with sheer delight.
They argue of pearls and who found the best,
But everyone knows it's the jokes that impress!

A lobster popped up with a wink and grin,
Said, "I once wore a hat made of tin!"
The shrimp chimed in with a cheeky jest,
"You think you're fancy? I'm better dressed!"

In a tight circle, they swap their tall tales,
Of lost sandals and floating gales.
With laughter echoing through the bay,
These crusty friends spice up the day!

So whether they boast or tell a fib,
Their ocean humor is quite the rib!
For treasures might be a glittering shell,
But the laughter they share is worth more than well!

Reflections of a Deep-Sea Collector

In my submarine, where bubbles gleam,
I collect oddities—what a dream!
A rubber duck with a pink bow tie,
And sea glass shards that seem to fly!

I found a fork that once belonged,
To a pirate singing an off-key song.
A patchwork quilt made of floating things,
And a fish that insists on wearing rings!

Each item's got a quirky tale,
Like mermaids playing with hammers and nails.
I laugh at the antics of these weird finds,
That glide through the waves like amused minds!

So join me now in this underwater mess,
With goofy relics, I must confess.
For every bobble and lost delight,
Is a giggle that bubbles both day and night!

Shades of the Ancient Mariner

Beneath the waves, a secret dance,
A sunken ship with a pirate's chance.
The fish all giggle, they poke and prod,
As clumsy crews find their lost facades.

A treasure chest filled with rusty spoons,
And jellyfish wearing goofy hats and tunes.
The captain's wig, a seaweed crown,
Each fish a jester, never a frown.

Octopus playing chess with a crab,
While dolphins laugh, waving a ragged slab.
What is the prize, if not the good cheer?
A merry plunder with a frozen beer!

So raise a glass to the depths below,
Where laughter bubbles and currents flow.
For while they seek gold, we find what's bright,
An ocean of giggles tucked out of sight!

Beneath Celestial Waters

Under the sea, stars twinkle bright,
But they're just fish playing in the night.
A sea otter slides with a splashy grin,
While a clam rolls its eyes, where to begin?

Shells sing songs of a dramatic flair,
As turtles breakdance without a care.
Flamboyant seaweed sways with style,
Even the shrimps can't help but smile.

Dolphins host parties with snacks from the deep,
As squids paint murals while others just sleep.
The treasures found, not just silver or gold,
But laughter and tales that are ever retold.

So next time you gaze at the glittering waves,
Remember the fun in the watery braves.
For beyond the treasure lurks joy in the tides,
A funny adventure where mirth never hides!

The Heartbeat of the Tides

The waves whisper secrets, in frothy delight,
With fish in tuxedos, all manners of fright.
A seahorse plays music, a conch for a drum,
While crabs do the cha-cha, oh what a hum!

Starfish trade gossip, with shells for a phone,
Each giggle a bubble, as laughter has grown.
Anemones tickle the snouts of the whales,
While eels share puns about circuits and trails.

The clattering clams clap a chorus of cheers,
While jellyfish float by, sharing their fears.
What's hidden beneath in this watery floor?
Just fun and games, and maybe some more!

So dive in the waves, embrace the surprise,
For fortune lies not in diamonds or ties.
But in laughter and joy, that the sea so imparts,
The heartbeat of tides, and the song of our hearts!

Forgotten Recipes of the Sea

A cookbook of fish, with pages so damp,
Revealing old secrets, from each ocean camp.
Crabby delights that come with a twist,
And tales of the flounder that surely persist.

The mermaids are chefs with a flair for the snazzy,
Whipping up flavors that make you feel jazzy.
"Saltwater soup or the seaweed surprise?"
Each dish is a laughter that tickles your eyes.

From clam chowder jokes to sardine pies,
Where turtles serve tea and dolphins are wise.
The octopus rumbles, "Just add a pinch of fun!"
In kitchens of coral where all hearts run.

So dive in the feasting, with friends all around,
Where the laughter of dinner is the best prize found.
For who needs a fortune when flavors are free?
In this underwater feast, we find glee at sea!

www.ingramcontent.com/pod-product-compliance
Lightning Source LLC
Chambersburg PA
CBHW060134230426
43661CB00003B/417